This book is provided through a grant from

TARGET.

to The Hayner Public Library District
for the program
1000 Books Before Kindergarten

A Note to Parents

DK READERS is a compelling new program for beginning readers, designed in conjunction with leading literacy experts, including Dr. Linda Gambrell, Director of the School of Education at Clemson University. Dr. Gambrell has served on the Board of Directors of the International Reading Association and as President of the National Reading Conference.

Beautiful illustrations and superb full-color photographs combine with engaging, easy-to-read stories to offer a fresh approach to each subject in the series. Each DK READER is guaranteed to capture a child's interest while developing his or her reading skills, general knowledge, and love of reading.

The four levels of DK READERS are aimed at different reading abilities, enabling you to choose the books that are exactly right for your child:

Level 1 – Beginning to read
Level 2 – Beginning to read alone
Level 3 – Reading alone
Level 4 – Proficient readers

The "normal" age at which a child begins to read can be any-where from three to eight years old, so these levels are intended only as a general guideline.

No matter which level you select, you can be sure that you are help-ing your child learn to read, then read to learn!

LONDON, NEW YORK, MUNICH,
MELBOURNE, and DELHI

Produced by Southern Lights
Custom Publishing

For Dorling Kindersley
Publisher Andrew Berkhut
Executive Editor Andrea Curley
Art Director Tina Vaughan
Photographer Keith Harrelson

Reading Consultant
Linda Gambrell, Ph.D.

First American Edition. 2001
14 30 29 28 27 26
Published in the United States by
DK Publishing
345 Hudson Street, New York, New York 10014
028-XA001-Mar/2001

Published in Great Britain by Dorling Kindersley Limited.

Library of Congress Cataloging-in-Publication Data

Hayward, Linda.
A day in the life of a firefighter / by Linda Hayward.
1st American ed.
Audience:"Level 1, pre-school-grade 1."
p. cm. -- (Dorling Kindersley readers)
ISBN:978-0-7894-7366-0(hc)
ISBN:978-0-7894-7365-3(pb)

1. Fire extinction--Juvenile literature. [1. Fire fighters. 2. Fire
extinction. 3. Occupations.] I. Title. II. Series.

TH9148 .H39 2001
628.9'25--dc21   00-055538

Printed and bound in China by L. Rex Printing Co., Ltd.

The characters and events in this story are fictional and do not repre-
sent real persons or events. The author would like to thank Fire Chief
Frank Kovarik for his help. Special thanks to Fire Chief Robert Ezekiel,
City of Mountain Brook Fire Department, Mountain Brook, Alabama.

All other images © Dorling Kindersley
For further information see: www.dkimages.com

Discover more at
www.dk.com

DK READERS

BEGINNING
TO READ
1

A Day in the Life of a Firefighter

Written by Linda Hayward

DK
DK Publishing

Rob Green packs clean
clothes and says good-bye
to his family.
Rob is a firefighter.

8:00 a.m.

At the fire station
he puts his clothes
in a locker.
Rob is on duty
for 24 hours.

Chief Myers gives the firefighters jobs for the day.

In case of fire, Rob is on rescue. Rob gets other jobs, too. Check the hoses and the nozzles. Cook supper.

nozzle

"A new restaurant needs to be inspected this morning," Chief Myers says. "And a second-grade class is coming to visit after lunch."

Rob checks. Nozzles
change the way the water
sprays out of the hose. All
of the nozzles are working.

Pete turns on the engine. Is there enough gas?

Luis checks the oil level.

10:30 a.m.

EXIT

Rob and Pete inspect the restaurant. Is the fire exit light on?

fire exit

Where is the fire
extinguisher?

Do the sprinklers
work?

sprinkler

12:00 p.m.

It is lunch time.

Luis tells about
his fishing trip.
He caught enough to share.
Later, Rob will cook
the fish for supper.

1:30 p.m.

siren

Ms. Hill's class visits the fire
station. Where is the siren?

Rob shows the class what he wears to a fire. This is the air pack.

air pack

"Remember!" Pete says. "In a room full of smoke, stay near the floor."

It is almost supper time. Rob cooks in the fire house kitchen.

Fried fish for twelve hungry firefighters!

6:00 p.m.

Ring! Ring! Ring!

The fire alarm goes off.
Everyone scrambles!

Rob is ready
to go.

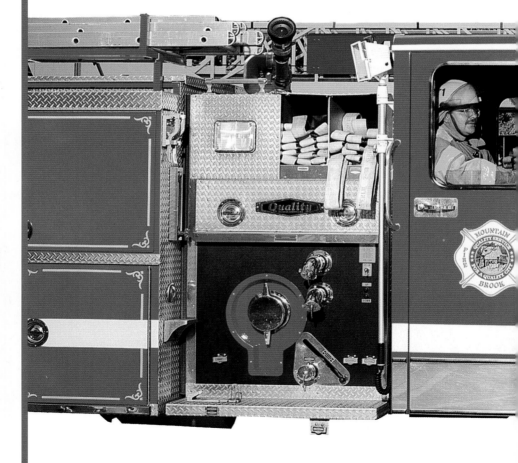

The fire engine
roars out of the station.
EEE–I I I, EEE–I I I
goes the siren.

6:10 p.m.

Pete puts on his mask
and takes the attack
line to the door.
He waits.

mask

Rob is on rescue.
Michelle's dog Pickles is still in
the house!

Rob goes in first.
He hears a bark.

He finds
Pickles in
the den.

Rob takes Pickles
to Michelle.

Pete has a radio inside
his helmet. Attack line
one—Go!

helmet

Pete goes in. Soon
water will rush out of
the hose.

The fire is out!

Rob folds
the hose.

hose

Luis helps with
the cleanup.

8:00 p.m.

The chief reports—
the house is safe now.

Back at
the station,
everything
is cleaned.

The hose,
the truck...
the firefighters!

10:45 p.m.

Rob cooks again!
At last the firefighters get to eat
their fish dinner. Then it is time
for bed.

Rob sleeps at the station.
Before he falls asleep,
Rob thinks about
Michelle and Pickles.

He smiles.
He has the best job
in the world!

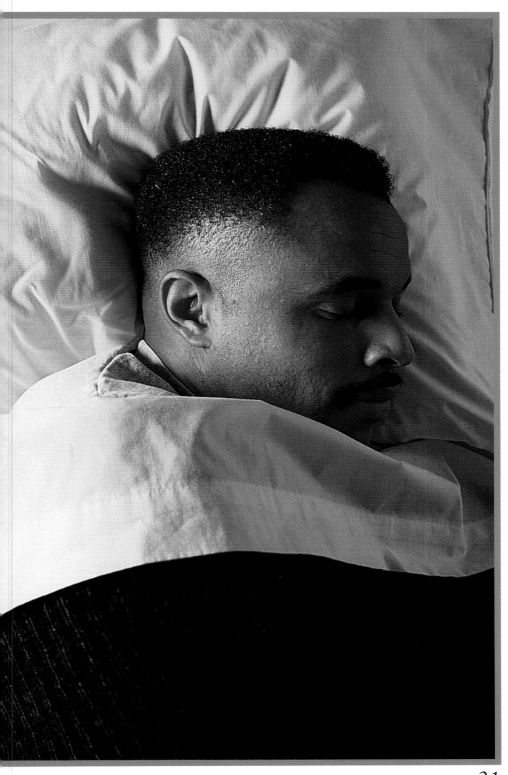

Picture word list

nozzle
page 6

air pack
page 15

EXIT

fire exit
page 10

mask
page 20

sprinkler
page 11

helmet
page 24

siren
page 14

hose
page 26